The *most* *excellent* book of
dress up

Moe Casey

COPPER BEECH BOOKS
BROOKFIELD, CONNECTICUT

© Aladdin Books Ltd
1997
Designed and produced by
Aladdin Books Ltd
28 Percy Street
London
WIP 0LD

*First published in the
United States in 1997 by*
Copper Beech Books,
an imprint of
The Millbrook Press
2 Old New Milford Road
Brookfield, CT 06804

Editor
Sarah Levete
Design
David West Children's
Book Design
Designer
Robert Perry
Illustrator
Rob Shone

Printed in Belgium

Library of Congress Cataloging-
in-Publication Data
Casey, Moe.
Dress up / Moe Casey ; illustrated
by Rob Shone.
p. cm. — (The most excellent
book of—)
Includes index.
Summary: Presents a variety of
costumes for all types of
occasions, suggesting how to
design, make, and use them.
ISBN 0-7613-0550-5 (lib. bdg.).
— ISBN 0-7613-0575-0 (pbk.)
1. Children—Costume—Juvenile
literature. 2. Children's clothing–
–Juvenile literature. [1. Costume.]
I. Shone, Rob, ill. II. Title.
III. Series.
TT633.C37 1997   96-48290
646.4'78—dc21   CIP
                         AC

CONTENTS

INTRODUCTION

Throughout history, people across the world have dressed in costumes for different purposes. Nations and races can be identified by their dress. Disguises allow people to act out different characters – court jesters were allowed

to say things to kings that other people would have been punished for. Dressing up continues to be fashionable at masquerades *(above right)*, carnivals *(above left)*, festivals *(below right)*, and parties. This book gives you the chance to make imaginative costumes using easily available materials. Try out different characters and think of some designs of your own.

As you read the book, look for these symbols:
★ *tells you what specific materials and equipment you need for the costume.*
✔ *gives you tips on how to perfect your costume and how to act out a character to suit your outfit.*

Different MATERIALS

Start collecting different and unusual materials.

★ *Collect old wrapping paper; food packaging; bottle tops; straws; bubble wrap; colored, plastic tops; cardboard boxes; plastic bottles; old rubber gloves; old clothes or pieces of material such as netting, fake fur, and felt; scarves, swimming caps and goggles, and baseball caps. You may need to buy: colored cellophane, tissue, and crepe paper; Velcro; wadding or foam (from a craft store). Don't worry if you don't have a particular item – most of the materials can be replaced – just think of an alternative.*

Examples of the types of materials that you can collect and use.

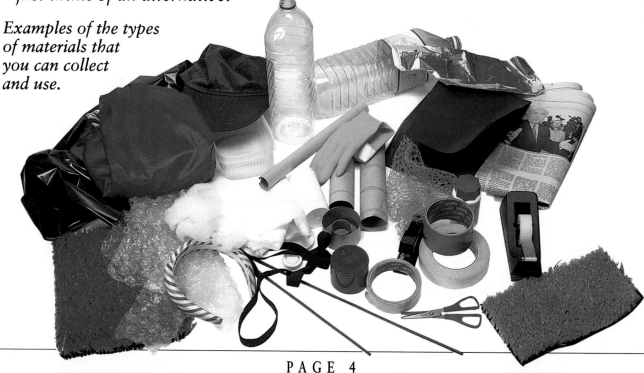

Safety first

• Use nontoxic glue and nontoxic acrylic paint • Be careful when you use scissors – if you have difficulty, ask an adult to help • Avoid putting glitter near your eyes • When you staple things, put some tape behind the sharp edges of the staple • Make sure your face is never covered completely by plastic or foam • If you are uncomfortable in a costume, take it off and make some alterations •

★ *Have the following on hand for each costume: scissors; stapler and staples; glue; adhesive tape; parcel tape or masking tape; ruler; needle and thread; paintbrush.*

The long edges of a cardboard box are called the front and back; the short edges are called the sides. If you need to cut out the base of a box and your box has open flaps, just cut off the flaps.

Cleaning up

Cover your work area with newspaper and clean up when you have finished.

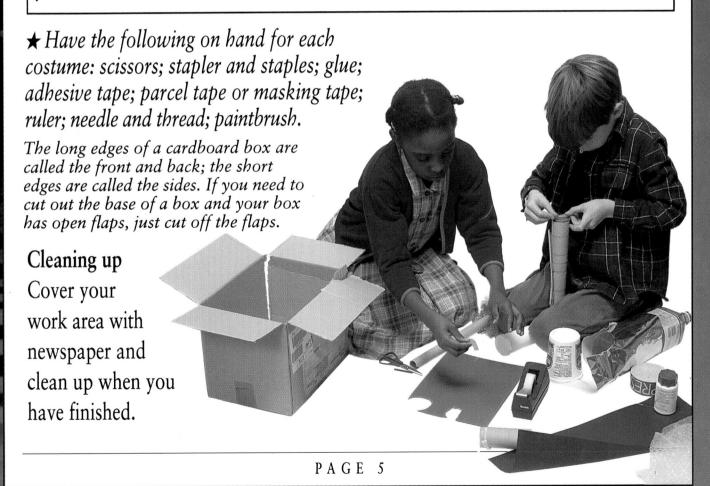

Putting things TOGETHER

Simple techniques you may need for some costumes:

Pattern-making template

To make a pattern from a grid, cover paper or cardboard with 1-inch-squared boxes *(left)*, or buy paper printed with 1-inch squares. Copy the pattern on the grid in the costumemaking instructions by matching the pattern on the squares with your squared paper *(below)*. This will enlarge it. Cut out the pattern.

Template

Use tracing paper to copy your grid pattern onto cardboard. Trace the outline with pencil; turn the tracing paper over (pencil side face-down on the grid); trace through the original line. Lift the tracing paper off; draw over the faint outline, and cut out. Draw around this template to make other copies.

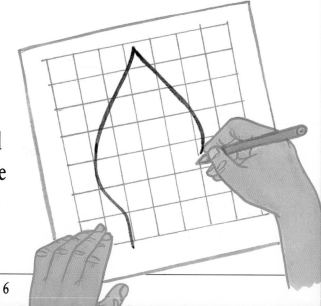

Scoring

This is when you drag the point of the scissors along a straight line next to a ruler *(right)*. Scoring cuts cardboard just on the surface, making it easier to bend. This is used on the "candy" *(see pages 10-11)*.

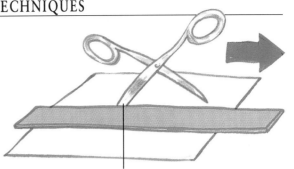

Drag the point of the scissors along the edge of the ruler.

Right side

Oversewing

This is sewing over two edges. Place two pieces of fabric with their right sides together. The needle is put through both pieces and the thread pulled tight and then repeated *(left)*. This is used on the "alien" *(see pages 22-23)*.

Wrong side

Gathering stitch

This is a large, flat running stitch that is pulled in to form gathers *(right)*. This is used for the "superhero" cape *(see pages 18-19)*.

✔ *If you find a technique difficult, ask an adult for help. Read through the instructions carefully before you begin making your costume.*

Gathers form as the stitch is pulled.

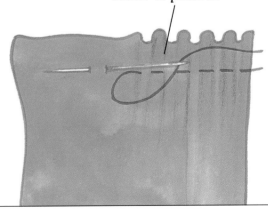

Beautiful BUTTERFLY

Flap your wings gracefully like a butterfly!

★ *Large cardboard box approx. 22 in. x 15 in.; glitter; newspaper; tissue paper; paint; 2 pieces of 0.5-in.-wide elastic.*

1 Cut the front and back out of the cardboard box.

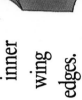

2 Draw a half-butterfly wing shape (*right*) onto newspaper; make sure it will cover the top half of your body. Cut this out and trace around it on the two pieces of cardboard. Cut out a pair of wings.

3 Lay the wings next to each other. Add a little water to some glue. Brush this onto the front of the wings. Cover each wing with tissue paper. Glue on crushed tissue paper.

4 Cut a strip of cardboard to cover the inner wing edges.

Cotton ball dipped in glitter

Elastic strips for your arm

✔ *Why not make a caterpillar costume to wear before you are transformed into a butterfly? Look at some pictures or photos of caterpillars to give you ideas.*

5 Score and fold down the center. Glue and tape it to the back of the wings.

6 Paint the back of the wings. Staple the elastic strips onto the front of the wings. Your arms will fit through here.

7 Place the wings on the newspaper and paint glue onto the edge of the wings. Sprinkle a little glitter around, shake off the excess. Repeat this a few times.

Headband and springs

8 Ask an adult to help you put your wings on. Wear colored leggings and a leotard or sweater.

★ *For the antennae, attach two painted pipe cleaners, straws, or springs to an old headband. Stick a cotton ball on top of each. Paint them with glue and dip them into a bag of glitter. Shake off the excess onto some newspaper and repeat the process.*

7

6

EXCELLENT CANDY COSTUME

Colorful CANDY

Smile sweetly...

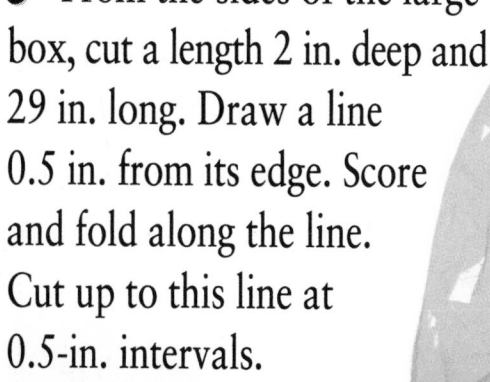

1 Cut a hole large enough for your head in the top of the small box. Cut out the base or its flaps. In the sides of the box, cut two shoulder grooves.

★ *A roll of colored cellophane; colored wrapping paper; small cardboard box; large cardboard box; colored paint; stiff paper.*

2 Cut two oval shapes from the front and back of the large box. Cover them with wrapping paper. Tape them to the front and back of the small box.

3 From the sides of the large box, cut a length 2 in. deep and 29 in. long. Draw a line 0.5 in. from its edge. Score and fold along the line. Cut up to this line at 0.5-in. intervals.

4 Paint this piece the color of the cellophane. Staple it together to form a circle. Glue and tape around the hole in the top of the small box.

5 Cut a piece of cardboard 2 in. deep and 35 in. long, to form a circle. Tape it around the bottom of both ovals.

6 Cut a length of paper 29 in. long and 1 in. deep. Make pleats in the cellophane (0.5 in. deep and 0.5 in. apart). Staple and tape the pleats along the paper's edge. This is tricky so you may need to ask an adult to help you. Staple this around the cardboard circle (**4**). Leave a space in the front of the cellophane for your face. Repeat for the bottom of the candy, stapling the paper to the circle shape (**5**). Here, tape the sides of the cellophane together. Ask an adult to help you put it on.

✔ *Make sure your friends aren't tempted to unwrap you!*

NEVER cover your face with cellophane. Make sure you leave a gap.

EXCELLENT VAMPIRE BAT COSTUME

Vampire BAT

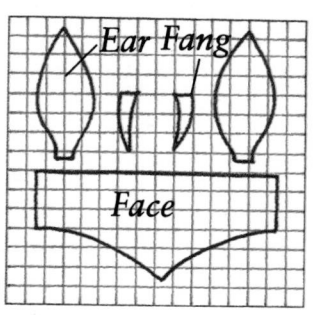

Ear Fang

Face

Bat around and terrify your friends as you go!

★ *Black baseball cap; black felt; black ribbon; black sweatsuit or black top and pants; black shoes; a large black plastic bag; needle and strong thread; red paint; grid paper; thin piece of foam.*

1 Copy the ear and face patterns from the grid. Fold the felt in half and cut out two ear shapes. Sew the matching ear shapes together to make them double thickness. Cut out one face shape in black felt. Cut out foam fangs.

2 Cut 2 slits , 1.5 in. from the top of the baseball cap. Pleat the base of the ears; place one through each slit. Turn the cap inside out; sew ears to it.

3 Glue or stitch the felt face onto the back of the baseball cap. This is now the front. If glued, allow to dry.

Wrist and elbow ties

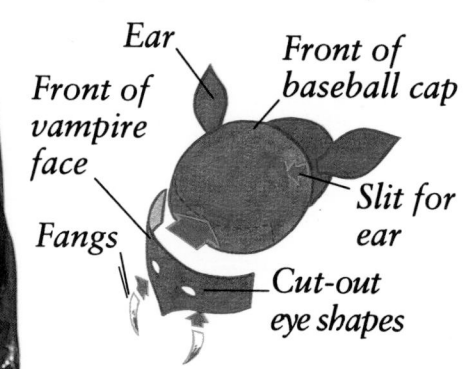

Ear

Front of baseball cap

Front of vampire face

Slit for ear

Fangs

Cut-out eye shapes

4 Try it on. Ask an adult to mark where your eyes are. Take the cap off and cut out eye holes. Paint the foam fangs vampire-red. Glue to the inside of the face-shaped felt.

5 Cut along the top and one edge of the plastic bag. Lay the bag on the floor. Copy the curved cape shape and cut out your cape pattern from the bag. From the rest of the bag, cut out 8 strips each 1 in. long for the elbow and wrist ties.

6 To strengthen the cape, fold twice along the top edge of the plastic bag and staple. Staple the ties to the cape at wrist and elbow level. Staple ribbon to the back of the cape. Loosely tie the ribbon around your neck. Get help to tie your cape at the wrists and elbows.

Wear black clothes underneath

✔ *Put on your bat cap. Make vampire noises as you flap away!*

Ribbon

Ties for wrists and elbows

5

6

DINER

Wear your best smile. Have a nice day!

★ Grid sheet; a large box; 3 feet of checked cloth or an old sheet painted with fabric paint; a paper plate; a baseball cap; an old bath sponge or foam; piece of elastic for bow tie; stick-on Velcro.

1 Cut out the base of the box and a half-circle from the top. From the base, cut a length 30 in. long and 3.25 in. deep. This is for your waistband.

2 Score a line 2.5 in. from the longer, top edge. Along the middle, cut up to the scored edge at 1-in. intervals. Bend the scored edges upward. These edges fit under the semicircle (step **1**). Tape in place.

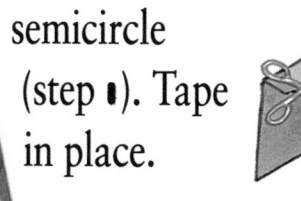

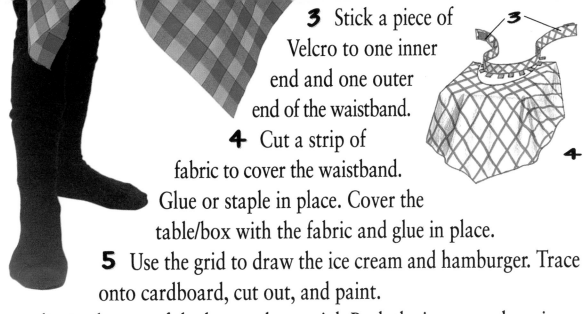

3 Stick a piece of Velcro to one inner end and one outer end of the waistband.

4 Cut a strip of fabric to cover the waistband. Glue or staple in place. Cover the table/box with the fabric and glue in place.

5 Use the grid to draw the ice cream and hamburger. Trace onto cardboard, cut out, and paint.

6 Cut two slits in the top of the box and material. Push the ice cream base in one. Make a slit in the paper plate and push the burger through. Push this into the other table slit. Cut up an old bath sponge to make fries.

7 Cover the front of the baseball cap with some leftover material. Glue or sew in place. Make a bow tie by folding over a piece of the material into a rectangular shape. Pleat it in the center and wrap a narrow piece of material around it. Thread some elastic behind the narrow piece. Ask an adult to tie it loosely around your neck and to attach the table at the back. Hold the table from underneath.

Ice cream sundae

Burger

✔ *Do you have an order book and pen?*

Scary SKELETON

What a lot of bones!

★ *A large sheet of cardboard (not too thick); a large grid sheet; paper fasteners; black paint or black marker; white and black face paints; black elastic; ribbon or tape; black turtleneck and leggings; black gloves.*

I Use the grid reference to make an enlarged skeleton pattern. You may need an adult to help you.

2 The bones are cut out using a template *(see page 6)*. Draw around the template of one bone to make the other bones – you will need two of each of the bones to make two arms and two legs.

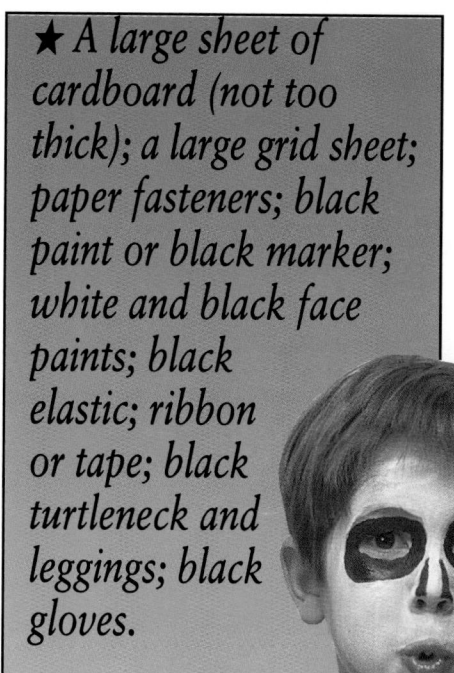

Ribcage and pelvis

3 For the ribs and pelvis, cut the outer shape but mark out the gaps in between the bones with a black marker or paint.

4 Use the point of the scissors to make a hole, where the dots are marked.

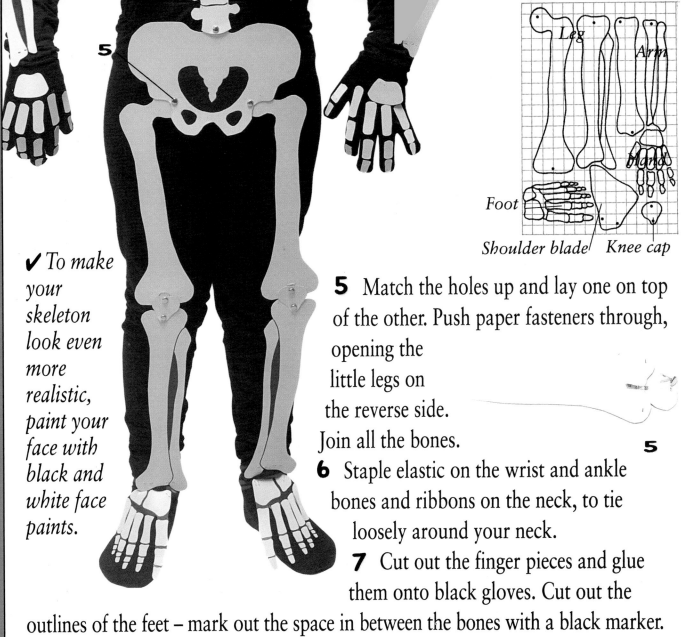

5

Leg

Arm

Hand

Foot

Shoulder blade   Knee cap

✔ To make your skeleton look even more realistic, paint your face with black and white face paints.

5 Match the holes up and lay one on top of the other. Push paper fasteners through, opening the little legs on the reverse side. Join all the bones.

6 Staple elastic on the wrist and ankle bones and ribbons on the neck, to tie loosely around your neck.

7 Cut out the finger pieces and glue them onto black gloves. Cut out the outlines of the feet – mark out the space in between the bones with a black marker. Attach some elastic at the heel and put them on top of your feet.

5

✔ Scrape your hair back with gel or wear a white headband

EXCELLENT SUPERHERO COSTUME

*Super*HERO

What superheroic deeds can you perform?

★ *Purple satin (3 ft. long, 55 in. wide); 2 fruit trays, from a supermarket; a wide belt; cotton tape, 1.5 in. wide and long enough to go around your neck; baseball cap; red acrylic paint; newspaper; stick-on Velcro; black elastic; rubber boot.*

1 Cut out one tray (as shown) for the front piece of your costume. For the headdress and boots, cut two corners off both trays.

2 From the other tray, cut two diagonal pieces for your wristbands.

Front of costume shape

Cut 2 corners from each tray

3 Put the pieces on some newspaper and paint them red on one side. Allow to dry and paint the other side.

4 Staple elastic to the wristbands and boot pieces (two corners from step **1**).

5 Staple the bottom of the front piece (**1**) to your belt.

Wrist piece

Front piece

6 Stick two Velcro pieces along the top.

7 Cut the satin (for the cape) 27.5 in. long, using the whole width of fabric. Sew a gathering stitch across the top; pull it in to 20 in.; stitch this to some cotton tape. Stick a piece of Velcro to each end of the cotton tape (this will attach to the Velcro on your front piece). To stiffen the bottom of the cape, lightly paint some glue along its bottom edge.

8 Staple some material to cover the baseball cap, the back of which will be the front. Staple a headdress piece onto either side and staple a center piece in the middle. With the elastic, attach the boot pieces to your rubber boots.

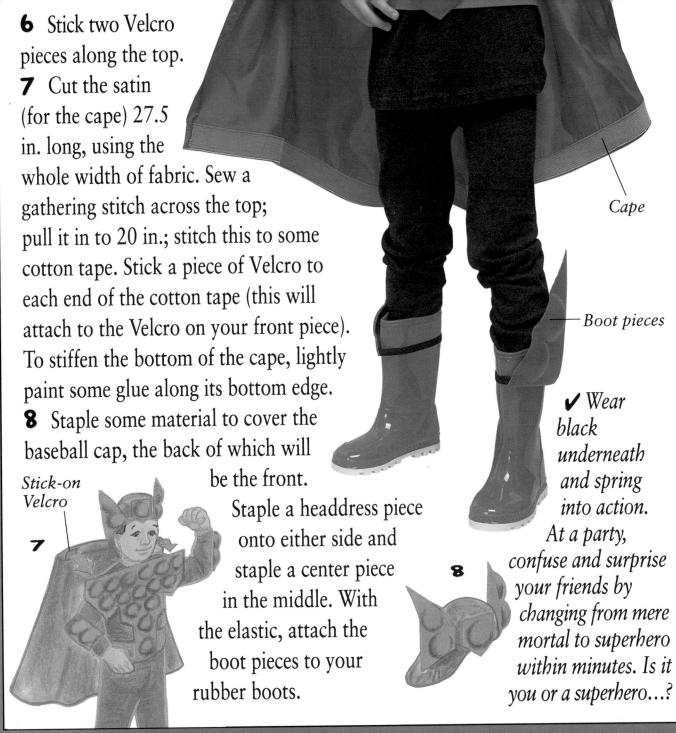

Cape

Boot pieces

Stick-on Velcro

7

8

✔ *Wear black underneath and spring into action. At a party, confuse and surprise your friends by changing from mere mortal to superhero within minutes. Is it you or a superhero…?*

EXCELLENT JELLYFISH COSTUME

Stinging JELLYFISH

Float around the party, stinging as you go.

Colander

★ *A colander; plastic tubing cut into 2 lengths of 3 ft. and 1 length of 6 ft. (from hardware stores); a sheet or strips of bubble wrap; 5 ft. x 5 ft. of wadding or foam, 0.5 in. thick; old yarn, thread, rope, or party throws; needle and thread; blue and green acrylic paints.*

1 Tape the 3-ft. tubes into a cross shape.

2 Put the colander upside down on a stool.

2

Tube taped around 4 points of cross.

Tape the top of the cross onto the colander. Ask an adult to help you tape the 6-foot length of tubing around the bottom of the cross.

3 Place the wadding over the frame. Attach it by sewing the wadding to one of the cross shape pieces of tubing. Use big stitches.

Make sure you have cut a hole for your face.

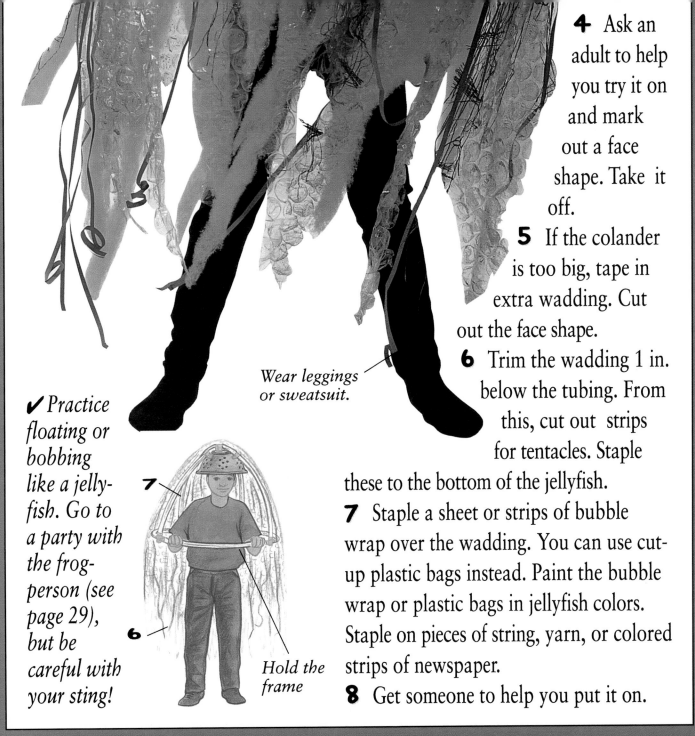

4 Ask an adult to help you try it on and mark out a face shape. Take it off.

5 If the colander is too big, tape in extra wadding. Cut out the face shape.

6 Trim the wadding 1 in. below the tubing. From this, cut out strips for tentacles. Staple these to the bottom of the jellyfish.

7 Staple a sheet or strips of bubble wrap over the wadding. You can use cut-up plastic bags instead. Paint the bubble wrap or plastic bags in jellyfish colors. Staple on pieces of string, yarn, or colored strips of newspaper.

8 Get someone to help you put it on.

Wear leggings or sweatsuit.

✔ *Practice floating or bobbing like a jellyfish. Go to a party with the frog-person (see page 29), but be careful with your sting!*

7

6

Hold the frame

EXCELLENT ALIEN COSTUME

Furry ALIEN

Alienate your friends!

Mask

1 Use the grid to cut out mask shape. Cut it out from the paper. Cut out eye holes. Staple bubble wrap behind eye holes.

2 Paint mask. Outline the eyes and edge, and paint dots on bubble wrap. Staple thin fabric strips or paper scraps

★ *Grid paper; piece of paper; a plastic bowl; 3 ft. of fur fabric or an old bedspread; 1.5 ft. of thin fabric cut into strips; two strips of wiro binding from old files or pipe cleaners; old skirt or piece of thin material; 2 pairs of rubber gloves; green and black paint.*

Ask an adult to help you put the mask and collar on.

onto the lower edge of the mask. Tape the mask onto the bowl.

3 Place 2 strips of fur fabric (4 in. wide) across the top of the mask on the bowl. Into these, insert and staple wiro binding (antennae) to the fabric. Tie on material scraps.

Tape mask to bowl

3

4 Cover the bowl with the fabric. Staple strips of material on the back.

5 Cut a curve shape from an old skirt or piece of material. Staple fabric strips to the edges. This is your collar and sleeves. Staple together at the end to make arm holes.

5

6 Make a long tube out of the rest of the fur fabric. Oversew with thread. Stitch at the top to gather in. Cut out an upside-down V shape from the bottom. Sew up the sides for the leg holes.

Feet   *Hands*

7 Stuff the fingers of one pair of rubber gloves with newspaper. Put on your feet like socks. Staple the last two fingers of the other pair of gloves onto the palm of the glove. Put two of your fingers in each of the alien fingers.

Elegant EGYPTIAN

Go back in time with this historical costume.

Sew yarn across the tape

2

1 Put the tights over your head (not your face). Tie the legs into a double knot. This is the wig base. Take it off; cut the tights off 2.5 in. away from the knot. Cut the cotton tape 1.5 in. longer than your head measurement from front to back.

2 Place the wool lengths on the cotton tape; sew the middle of the wool along the center of the tape. Stitch and glue this to the wig base.

3 Paint a gold line on the bottom edge of the crepe paper. When dry, ask an adult to wrap it around your waist, pleating it at the front, and to staple it together.

Attach with Velcro

4 Cut and paint 2 bracelets from gold cardboard, 3 in. deep and 6 in. long.

Snake shape

Collar

Put Velcro along the opening edge of the collar. When you put it on, bend it slightly flat, so it does not stick out.

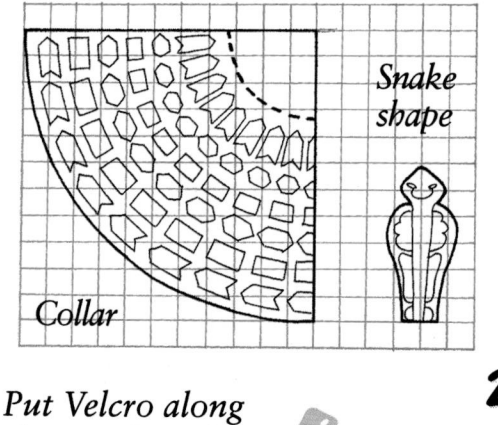

6

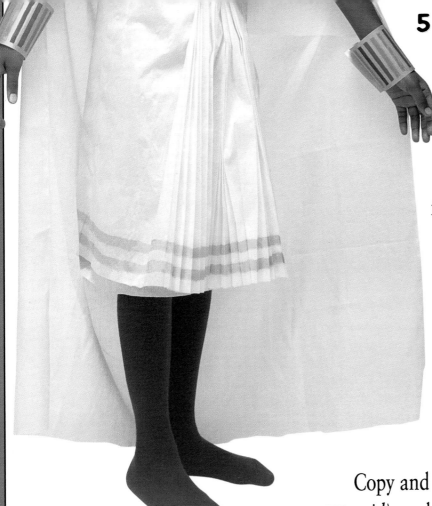

5 Copy the collar *(see grid)* onto plain cardboard; cut out. Trace this 4 times (to make a circle) onto gold cardboard.

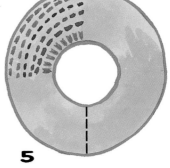

Attach with Velcro

Cut out; cut 1 side for the back opening; cut a circular hole for your neck. Paint.

6 Ask an adult to measure your head with the wig on. Cut a headband from the gold cardboard, 1.5 in. wide and 1 in. longer than the measurement. Decorate it. Copy and cut out the snake shape *(see grid)*, and decorate. Staple this to the front of the headband.

7 Loosely tie white muslin at the neck, under your collar.

★ 3.5-ounce ball of thick black yarn cut into 32-in. lengths; old pair of black tights; 1.5-in.-wide black cotton tape; needle and thread; 4 feet of white muslin; grid sheet; white crepe paper; 1 large sheet of gold cardboard; paints; Velcro.

Programmed ROBOT

What have you been programmed to do?

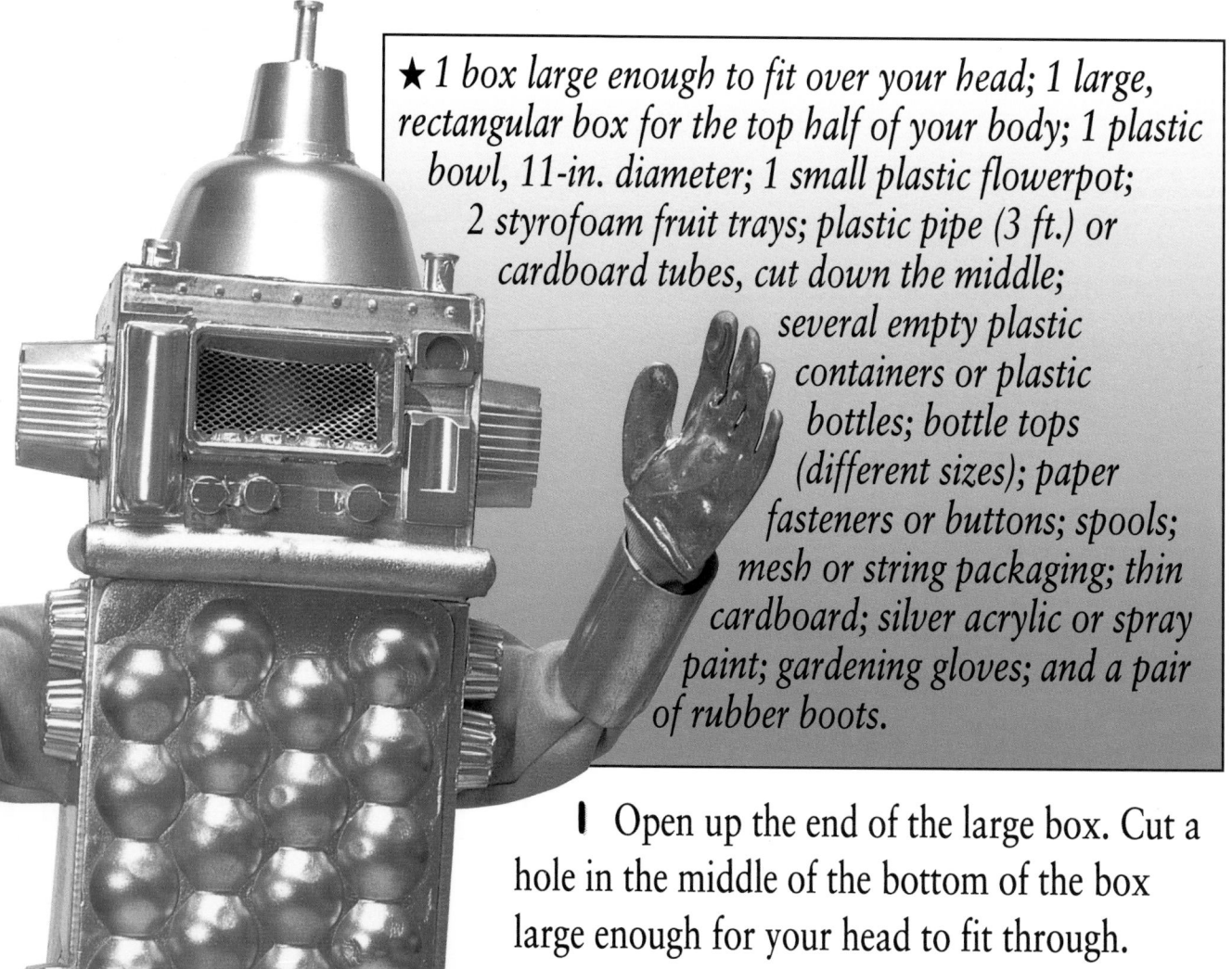

★ *1 box large enough to fit over your head; 1 large, rectangular box for the top half of your body; 1 plastic bowl, 11-in. diameter; 1 small plastic flowerpot; 2 styrofoam fruit trays; plastic pipe (3 ft.) or cardboard tubes, cut down the middle; several empty plastic containers or plastic bottles; bottle tops (different sizes); paper fasteners or buttons; spools; mesh or string packaging; thin cardboard; silver acrylic or spray paint; gardening gloves; and a pair of rubber boots.*

1 Open up the end of the large box. Cut a hole in the middle of the bottom of the box large enough for your head to fit through.

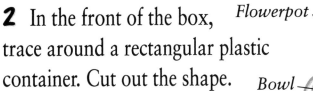

Flowerpot — Spool

Bowl —

Cartons /

2 In the front of the box, trace around a rectangular plastic container. Cut out the shape.

3 Trace around the plastic bowl on the top of the box and cut out the shape. Tape the flowerpot onto the top of the plastic bowl and tape a spool on top of that.

4 Insert this through the inside of the box, pushing through the hole in the top. Tape firmly in place.

5 Tape and glue bottle tops and spools either side of the bowl.

6 Cut the base off the rectangular plastic container. Tape some mesh or string packaging over the hole. Tape some bottle tops along the side of the container. Paint it silver. This is your eye hole. Decorate the top edge of the front of the box by inserting paper fasteners and sticking on buttons and bottle tops.

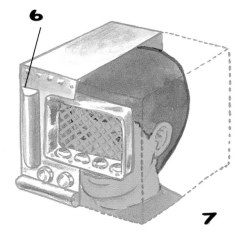

7 Insert your eye hole into the cut-out rectangular shape (**2**) and tape it into place.

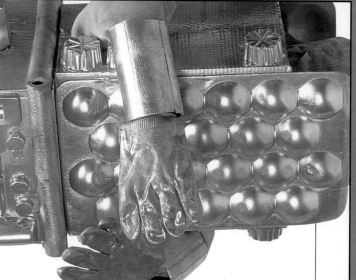

8 Cut the plastic pipe in half and glue around the bottom edge of the box – you could also use toilet paper rolls cut in half through the middle.

9 Tape the side edge of the box (**11**). Tape some flat containers onto the sides. If you use rounded shapes, trace and cut around them on the sides and then insert from inside the box and tape in place.

10 From one side of the large rectangular box, cut out a hole for your head (same size as **10**). Cut out all of the opposite side. Turn the box to stand on its cut-out side, with the head hole uppermost. Cut out arm holes.

11 Glue the fruit trays onto the front and back, and plastic containers on the sides with the armholes. Paint everything silver.

12 For the arms, use cardboard to make cylinders. Staple together and paint silver.

13 Paint the gardening gloves and boots silver.

14 Ask an adult to help you put on your costume.

*Frog*PERSON

Go underwater as a frogperson!

> ★ *2 large plastic bottles; pipe or corrugated tubing; black elastic; old plastic bath mat; swimming goggles; piece of cardboard; silver paint.*

Wear sweat-suit or leggings and a leotard.

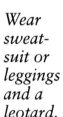

1 Tape bottles together. Attach plastic tubing onto one bottle neck. Cut a piece off the end and tape this to the other bottle top. Tape this to the large piece of tubing; paint it all silver.

2 For the mouthpiece, cut a hole in the center of the cardboard. Place the free length of piping through this. Paint it silver and bend the cardboard over slightly.

3 Cut out two flipper shapes from the bath mat. Stick some Velcro at the back and attach over bare feet. Ask an adult to tie some elastic between the bottles to attach the outfit to your body.

4 Get your goggles on. Get diving!

Other IDEAS

From pirates to mice, try some more costumes.

> ★ *Use baseball caps, felt, and fur fabric to make fox, mouse, and elephant costumes. Use fruit trays for a carnival headdress. Use felt, a plastic bottle, and aluminum foil for the pirate.*

Use the grid patterns for the fox and mouse. Follow stage **2** of the vampire bat for ears *(see page 12)*.

Fox

1 Stitch the fur fabric ears onto the fur fabric headband shape *(see grid)*. Staple these in place on the back of the baseball cap. Stick some cardboard behind the ears to make them stand up.

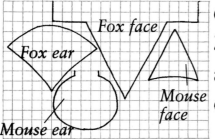

2 Cut straws in half and staple to nose shape – cut a cotton ball in half. Paint this black and staple it onto the fur fabric.

Mouse

Follow the steps for the fox, but use gray and pink felt, without a headband shape.

Carnival

Cut a fruit tray into five segments, lengthwise (follow the curve of the shapes); staple onto a piece of cardboard. Tape and stitch the cardboard to the headband; decorate brightly.

Elephant

Cut out thin foam ears and attach to the side of a gray baseball cap. Stitch some ducting (available form hardware stores) onto the back of the baseball cap – or you can use a "slinky" type toy to make the trunk.

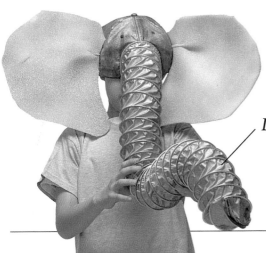

Ducting

Pirate *(see cover)*

Make an eye patch out of black felt, and attach it with elastic. Make a hook out of twisted aluminum foil, inserted into the top of a cut-off plastic bottle, painted black. Wear jeans and a T-shirt.

Dress up WORDS

Gathering stitch This is a large flat stitch used to form gathers.

Grid Squared paper which helps you to copy and enlarge a pattern.

Nontoxic A substance that is not poisonous.

Oversewing This is when you sew over two edges.

Scoring This is when you drag scissors across cardboard without cutting it.

Template An outline shape that you draw around to give you an exact copy.

INDEX

All costumes designed and made by Moe Casey except for cover, both: David West. Photographs by Roger Vlitos except for page 3, top left and bottom right: Eye Ubiquitous; top right: James Davis Travel Photography.

What to do NEXT

If you have enjoyed making costumes why not try to make your own costume designs. There are lots of other books in libraries about design and costume-making to give you ideas.